C000002845

THE HEALING POWER OF LAUGHTER

GAMELI ACOLATSE

ISBN: 978-9988-3-4639-3

Published by:
P.O. BOX BT 626
Tema-Ghana
+233(0) 244 644 893
+233(0) 506 707 225

For your personal copy of The Healing Power
of Laughter or for additional copies Kindly
contact author: +233 0244 644 893
Email: gacole3@gmail.com

DEDICATION
This book is dedicated to God almighty.

My prayer is that God will provide me with help and resources carry out this mandate by reaching out to many through this foundation.

TABLE OF CONTENTS

PREFACE

Children, they say, laugh 300 times a day while adults, 10% of that in a week. The outcome of this scarcity in adult life has resulted in a lot of stress related illnesses, premature aging and premature deaths. The kind of life we have chosen has more serious effects than we know. If laughter increases blood flow, boosts the immune system, lowers high PB, reduces pain, gives you a hearty and positive outlook to life, just imagine the harm we cause when we deprive ourselves of joy and laughter.

Much of this will go away if we just learn how to deal with stress properly. One of the greatest stress relievers God's given us is laughter. Laughter is like taking medicine according to the Bible. It does not only make you feel better but actually releases healing to your entire being; spirit, soul and body. Laughter, whether fake or real, restores and rejuvenates what the pressures of life take from you.

Most people today don't laugh as much as they should. They don't factor recreation, fun and laughter into their too busy schedules. They're too stressed up to have any fun but we need to get back in balance. Life is not supposed to be all work and no play. You need to develop your sense of humor by looking for opportunities to laugh. Scriptures say God laughs and has given us this ability to enable us to live and stay healthy. Therefore, train yourself to laugh more especially during difficult times.

Don't allow the pressures of this life to stress you and steal your joy. It is possible you haven't had a hearty laugh for years hence; your laughter is rusty. It needs to be overhauled and refilled and then you will have energy to laugh more often. Ensure that you don't lose the child on the inside of you. Getting older doesn't mean we should be droopy, grumpy and depressed. You need to revive the child within and see life on the lighter side as a child would.

It is healthy to have fun. I chanced upon a write up that revealed that one of the common ingredients of people who live beyond 90 years isn't about engaging in physical exercises or following a routine or regular diet but they being extremely joyful people. Decide now; live happily and laugh heartily!

Chapter One

GOD FACTORED IN LAUGHTER DURING THE CREATION OF MAN

Let the fields and their crops burst out with joy!

Let the trees of the forest sing for joy.
Psalm 96:12

Create Your Eden

Some people equate laughter to lack of seriousness especially when we are desperate, frustrated or seem to be failing but there is more to laughter than you can appreciate. Right from the beginning of creation, God created a garden as man's dwelling place. God didn't place man who He created in His image and likeness in the jungle but in a well-planned, esthetic and serene environment. There was a river flowing through Eden which had four tributaries that watered the garden and kept it green all year round. One of the rivers had the best gold and other costly stones you can find on earth.

Like any other gardener, God was very intentional in making sure that the scenery harmonized purely for man's enjoyment. Hence; in Genesis 2:9, we are told that:

And out of the ground the LORD God made every tree grow that is pleasant to the sight and good for food.

What is pleasant to the eyes can easily bring joy, smiles and laughter to the one adoring the scenery. You can deduct from the verse above that God wasn't only concerned about or interested in supplying us with food or our needs but a beautiful landscape, a very serene environment, a place that inspired joy, pleasure and laughter.

Initially, the Creator factored in rest, joy, peace, pleasure when He designed a habitat for man and where God maintained fellowship with the pride of all His creation. Note that Eden was Adam's home and office. A homey environment is always welcoming. No matter where you live, you can create that kind of space where you find joy in the simple but well selected flowers, pots, vases, etc. in your house. Plants can grow anywhere; even in pots, kitchen or your bedroom. You can have pets or create a sanctuary where different kinds of birds can fly by just to pay you a visit.

Thus, home isn't a place you hurriedly leave or flee from but a place to rest and take in all the physical beauty and the sweet fragrance from the flowers of the budding trees just at a glance and also enjoy the early morning chirps, trills, rattles and croaks from those birds you never imagined existed.

Life today can be just mechanical and hardly would one pause to enjoy nature. It is as though you will be left behind by the super speed world system with its misplaced definition of success. Adam's office was in the garden of Eden. He worked in a friendly environment while savoring the beautiful scenery now and then. That could have also influenced his excellent output; the ability to name all the animals God had made and whatever name Adam gave to the creatures, was approved by God.

Today, our definition of work is rigid and the motive is to meet high targets and outperform our competitors. Some employers engage the worker for twelve hours every day and six days every week. They work long hours and earn peanuts. Incorporate sessions for relaxation for your employees because that's best practice.

Share in Jesus' Happiness

Never forget that God gave man everything He Himself loves and enjoys. The reason why Jesus Christ came to the earth as a normal human being was to restore to us the lost Eden. When the first man, Adam sinned, God ejected him from His presence because God couldn't accommodate sin. With the coming of the last Adam, who is Jesus Christ, also came the restoration of Eden (1Corinthians 15:45-49). The last Adam is offering everything the first Adam lost.

However, if the born again believer doesn't live by faith he or she would certainly miss the rich and beautiful life of peace, joy and laughter God has imbued in us by

His Spirit and by nature. We cannot allow the pressures of this world to stifle the fruit of the Holy Spirit especially the love, peace, joy within us:

But the fruit of the Spirit is love, joy, peace, longsuffering, kindness, goodness, faithfulness, gentleness, self-control. Against such there is no law.
Galatians 5:22-23

It was in Nazareth that Jesus Christ presented His manifesto; a messianic prophecy from Isaiah 61:

The Spirit of the LORD is upon Me,
Because He has anointed Me
To preach the gospel to the poor;
He has sent Me to heal the brokenhearted,
To proclaim liberty to the captives
And recovery of sight to the blind,
To set at liberty those who are oppressed;

To proclaim the acceptable year of the LORD."

Luke 4:18-19

Jesus Christ, our Lord, dealt with the very things that subjected man into slavery by the world's system and its standards whose architect is Satan. The doorway to liberty is faith hence; the good news which is the gospel is preached to the poor. There are many kinds and levels of poverty. It goes beyond physical or financial lack but spiritual, emotional, health related, etc. The worst kind of poverty is in the mind and can only be cured by paying heed to the gospel of Jesus Christ.

... the poor have the gospel preached to them.
Matthew 11:5

It calls for accepting or believing and most importantly, renewing or "renovating" of the mind. Poverty of any kind is a mind thing which can be cured by hearing and hearing the good news of Jesus Christ (Romans 10:17). Jesus also announced to us at the onset of His ministry that He is restoring to us the season of God's favor (jubilee). When Jesus was born, the shepherds heard a great company of angels singing:

Glory be to God in the highest and
on earth peace to men on whom his favor rests.
Luke 2:14-NIV

On earth, Jesus brought us peace and where there is peace, there is also joy and laughter. Peace has been given to those on whom His favor or grace rests. It is by

God's grace you have been saved; it is not by your works (Ephesians 2:8). Jesus Christ and the Holy Spirit reside in the believer; you are the temple of God and everything in this world that stifles laughter has been done away with by Jesus Christ. Below is the rest of the prophecy Jesus quoted as presented by Prophet Isaiah 61:2-3:

> *To proclaim the acceptable year of the LORD,*
> *And the day of vengeance of our God;*
> *To comfort all who mourn,*
>
> *To console those who mourn in Zion,*
> *To give them beauty for ashes,*
> *The oil of joy for mourning,*
> *The garment of praise for the spirit of heaviness;*
> *That they may be called trees of righteousness,*
> *The planting of the LORD, that He may be*
> *glorified."*

In the prophecy, Jesus Christ consoles those who sorrow in Zion. Zion is symbolic of the church or those in the church. Every spirit of heaviness that is projected against you in order to drain your oil of joy and laughter mustn't be entertained. In Luke, Jesus concluded the reading of His manifesto with this announcement which you must read aloud to yourself:

... "Today this Scripture is fulfilled in your hearing."
Luke 4:21

When was the Scripture (messianic prophecy) fulfilled? It is "today"; not yesterday or tomorrow but now! Jesus deals with today's issues. It is the reason why anything that could drain the oil of gladness has been preempted several centuries ago; just for you!

Chapter Two

LAUGHTER IS DIVINE

I also will laugh at your calamity;

I will mock when your terror comes

Proverbs 1:26

Find Rest for Your Soul

No matter the burden you carry or how difficult life has become, it is very necessary to make room and live at the lighter side of life. That kind of life resides in your relationship with Jesus Christ. He has offered you rest through exchange of yokes or burdens

> *Take My yoke upon you and learn from Me, for I am gentle and lowly in heart, and you will find rest for your souls.*
> *For My yoke is easy and My burden is light."*
> **Matthew 11:29-30**

He says, take His yoke, for it is easy and His burden is light. How do you do that? You can ask Jesus about the how and He will certainly help you. There are twists to everything life presents and the scriptures are very plain on how a child of God should respond to them. In John, Jesus tells us that:

> *These things I have spoken to you, that in Me you may have peace. In the world you will have tribulation; but be of good cheer, I have overcome the world."*
> **John 16:33**

It should rather surprise you if you don't experience troubles, trials and sorrows here on earth. The things that bring distress and frustrations abound on this earth however, the Lord says "be of good cheer" because He has overcome this world.

To be of good cheer, you must take courage, be confident, certain and undaunted because Christ has deprived the enemy of the power to harm you! Be cheerful, be of good spirit, make merry, be smiling, be lively and optimistic even when you have a deadline to meet, when failure stares you in the face, when you are diagnosed of a terminal disease or when the person you love the most deserts you.

James reveals that those various trying moments are like the nine months of pregnancy period of a woman. At the end of the period, you will give birth to some exceptional virtues. Hear what apostles James and Paul said about trials:

My brethren, count it all joy when you fall into various trials, knowing that the testing of your faith produces patience.
James 1:2

And not only that, but we also glory in tribulations, knowing that tribulation produces perseverance; and perseverance, character; and character, hope.
Romans 5:3-4

Paul also hinted that some virtues are developed during these difficult moments and they are the reason why you mustn't allow the weight of the burden to crush your spirit but you must rather "glory in tribulations". There are many things we can learn from Jesus Christ. How did He endure tribulations associated with the cross? The writer of Hebrews explains:

Therefore, we also, since we are surrounded by so great a cloud of witnesses, let us lay aside every weight, and the sin which so easily ensnares us, and let us run with endurance the race that is set before us,
looking unto Jesus, the author and finisher of our faith, who for the joy that was set before Him endured the cross, despising the shame, and has sat down at the right hand of the throne of God.
Hebrews 12:1-2

The weight of fear, unbelief, worries, anxiety, despair, etc. can slow you down. You are being asked to throw these off so you can run life's race. Jesus Christ didn't set His eyes on the cross but on the joy that was beyond the cross (Hebrews 12:2).

Little David Wins, the Giant Goliath Loses

Interestingly, David's focus was on the reward whoever eliminated Goliath was to receive. Goliath' military exploits, experience, stature and fame notwithstanding how youthful, the shepherd David was interested in marrying the king's daughter. The young man might have been dreaming of becoming King Saul's son in-law someday. God might have seen the humor in the entire battle. Scripture describes details of the two fighters. Just imagine you watching this on TV. Goliath appears first in his military attire; a veteran soldier seriously ready to take on his opponent. You can see that right from his appearance:

> *He was over nine feet tall!*
> *He wore a bronze helmet, and his bronze coat of mail weighed 125 pounds.*
> *He also wore bronze leg armor, and he carried a bronze javelin on his shoulder. The shaft of his spear was as heavy and thick as a weaver's beam, tipped with an iron spearhead that weighed 15 pounds.*
> *His armor bearer walked ahead of him carrying a shield.*
> **1 Samuel 17:4-7- NLT**

What a sight Goliath might have created being fully clothed in bronze. He didn't really look earthly but like those zombie figures. David entered the battleground; just a boy! He was looking more like a shepherd with zero protective gear and funnily or casually armed:

> *He picked up five smooth stones from a stream and put them into his shepherd's bag. Then, armed only with his shepherd's staff and sling, he started across the valley to fight the Philistine.*
> **1 Samuel 17:40 NLT**

The whole stage of this war was as a comedy yet, God was setting destinies free from oppression. It's not surprising that David said in Psalm 2:4, that God actually laughs at those proud, self-dependent, godless opponents wherever they are. God's sense of humor is evident during very serious occasions.

The difference between Saul and his soldiers and David was the mindset. Have the mind of Christ and don't waste the rare and highly spiritual seasons that are meant to build your faith up. If you fret or worry whenever Goliath appears, you will not see the loopholes or his weaknesses for a more mature assessment, precise strikes and victory.

Jesus Slept When the Storm Was Raging
There was a day Jesus and His disciples were in a boat, making their way to the other side of the Sea of Galilee.

This river was the very place Peter, Andrew, James and John did their fishing business. It might have been familiar terrain for the four. Do you know how we handle such grounds? We do so with much confidence, effortlessly and mostly, without giving the process a thought. We can easily walk through this terrain even if we are blindfolded.

Now, these veteran fishermen were steering the boat on this same river when:

> ... *a great windstorm arose, and the waves beat into the boat, so that it was already filling.*
> *But He was in the stern, asleep on a pillow. And they awoke Him and said to Him, "Teacher, do You not care that we are perishing?"*
> **Mark 4:37-38**

The whole episode may have lasted just some seconds or minutes and that brief time was enough to expose what faith those twelve disciples really had. Have you ever gone through an experience you thought the worst was about to happen? What did you do in the heat of the incident? What do you do when you remember how you reacted then? It is always good to look back and really laugh at yourself for being too fearful and overreacting. I don't think Jesus' disciples forgot that experience ever.

Interestingly God's sense of humor is clearly depicted when we, human beings feel edgy; thinking the worst is about to happen. There are times you see evil gather like dark clouds in the sky that's about to empty itself as a heavy rain storm. The schemes of God's enemies and for that matter our enemies device are treated like divine set ups and God just laughs at their futile plans and efforts.

God Loves to Handle the Bullies
Can you imagine God having a good laugh at His well-equipped, battle ready enemies?

> *Why do the nations rage,*
> *And the people plot a vain thing?*
>
> *The kings of the earth set themselves,*
> *And the rulers take counsel together,*
> *Against the LORD and against His Anointed, saying,*
> *"Let us break Their bonds in pieces*
> *And cast away Their cords from us."*
>
> **He who sits in the heavens shall laugh;**
> **The LORD shall hold them in derision.**
> **Psalms 2:1-4**

Psalm 2 is a Messianic prophecy which was fulfilled when the Roman empire and the Jewish leaders came together and crucified Jesus, the Anointed one. Paul said if the rulers of this age had known that their wicked plans were rather furthering and establishing the will of God for humanity, they wouldn't have crucified the Lord of glory (1Corinthians 2:8). God sits in heaven and laughs at these powers; whether physical or spiritual.

> *The wicked plots against the just,*
> *And gnashes at him with his teeth.*
>
> ***The Lord laughs at him,***
> ***For He sees that his day is coming.***
> **Psalms 37:12-13**
>
> *They return at evening,*
> *snarling like dogs,*
> *and prowl about the city.*
>
> *See what they spew from their mouths —*
> *they spew out swords from their lips,*
> *and they say, "Who can hear us?"*
>
> ***But you, O LORD, laugh at them;***
> ***you scoff at all those nations.***
> **Psalms 59:6-8 NIV**

When you are fretting, God is laughing because He knows that those wicked plans will amount to nothing. Conspiracies in the offices against the righteous are very real. Someone's promotion has been hindered for years by a jealous boss. You are being transferred just because you refused to condone the evil in the office environment. Though you qualified, you weren't given the position or the contract because of unfair competition or treatments. You are being persecuted because you are a Christian; God assured the Israelites to stand still and see the salvation of the Lord (Exodus 12:14). When God is done with the bullies, you'll have a cause to also laugh.

Why do you boast of evil, you mighty man?
Why do you boast all day long,
you who are a disgrace in the eyes of God?
Your tongue plots destruction;
it is like a sharpened razor,
you who practice deceit.

You love evil rather than good,
falsehood rather than speaking the truth.
Selah
You love every harmful word,
O you deceitful tongue!
Surely God will bring you down to everlasting ruin:

He will snatch you up and tear you from your tent;
he will uproot you from the land of the living.
Selah
The righteous will see and fear;
they will laugh at him, saying,
"Here now is the man
who did not make God his stronghold
but trusted in his great wealth
and grew strong by destroying others!"

Psalms 52:1-7-NIV

Have you thought about why God chooses to laugh at the efforts of those who fight Him or attempt to fight His children?

After the Israelites had left Egypt, they got to the bank of the Red Sea and camped there. Pharaoh had regretted letting the Israelites go so he marshaled his chariots and horsemen with the intention of bringing the children of Israel back into captivity. There are times Satan will stir up trouble because of the bright future God has packaged for you. The fact that you are held back in Egypt, God is working on your case and sooner, the glory of God will manifest fully in your life. However, begin to laugh now!

When the children of Israel lifted their eyes and saw the Egyptian army coming, they concluded that Pharaoh and his soldiers would have the upper hand. Pharaoh's soldiers were battle ready; equipped, swift and strong but God wasn't with them. In fear, the children of Israel even spoke about they preferring to die in Egypt as slaves than in the wilderness as liberated people.

The question is, why would God truncate His glory from manifesting fully in your life? A high price was paid for your salvation. It cost God His only begotten Son hence; it is not over yet. God would have whisked you straight to heaven the moment you got born again.

During the frenzy in the camp of the Israelites, God got to work immediately on His children's behalf; possibly enjoying every bit of it:

And the Angel of God, who went before the camp of Israel, moved and went behind them; and the pillar of cloud went from before them and stood behind them.
So it came between the camp of the Egyptians and the camp of Israel. Thus it was a cloud and darkness to the one, and it gave light by night to the other, so that the one did not come near the other all that night.
Exodus 14:19-20

Moses's rod was raised and then the Red Sea parted into two just for the Israelites to walk on the dry ground to the other side. Were they able to take in that rare miracle of sea parting? The sound of the parting waters and the mind-blowing panorama! God intervened when Moses' rod was raised. Learn to laugh in your pain! Maintain your joy because God doesn't rest or retire.

The Egyptians couldn't see what God was doing because there was a pillar of cloud and darkness on their side while wonderful things were happening on the side of the Israelites. Whoever is on God's side experiences amazing miracles. Psalms 126:1-3:

When the LORD brought back the captivity of Zion,
We were like those who dream.

Then our mouth was filled with laughter,
And our tongue with singing.
Then they said among the nations,
"The LORD has done great things for them."
The LORD has done great things for us,
And we are glad.

When the deliverance of God started rolling out, it was like a dream then the reality dawned on the people and they laughed so loud that even other nations; their neighbors heard it. Your neighbors will testify of this fact that God has indeed visited you and has done great things for you.

Understand that catching sight of your enemy doesn't indicate that he has gotten the upper hand. God wants you to witness their end, hence; he laughs at them to scorn. Their presence is just a set up and you should join in the laughter!

Chapter Three

HUMOR IN THE STORY OF ABRAHAM AND SARAH

And Sarah said, "God has made me laugh,

and all who hear will laugh with me."

Genesis 21:6

God Wants You to Always Laugh

The birth of Isaac will definitely make the news in our time and age! Can you imagine how the catchy headlines will read? You can also attempt composing a suitable headline for the birth of your Isaac! This divinely orchestrated miracle in the lives of the father of our faith is a template for God's covenant people because faith in God has no time limits.

However, the inability to bring forth children after marriage is one of the stressful periods in the lives of couples all over the world. The pressure to conceive or make babies and the fact that even science can't guarantee this has left beautiful marriage relationships either strained or broken. The "for better for worse" marriage vow has tested many marriage couples and has left behind broken marriages, broken hearts, broken homes and also in its trail are marital unfaithfulness, hurts and tears, emotional and physical abuses and many other painful experiences.

When Abram was ninety-nine years old, God changed his name to Abraham and Sarai, his wife's name to Sarah. The age difference between Abraham and Sarah was ten years. The new names indicated that they shall become parents of many nations and kings of people shall trace their lineage to this couple. All their married life, they had looked forward to having children especially when God encouraged them to change their names.

In a chat with Abraham, God hinted at giving Abraham and Sarah a son. Do you know how Abraham reacted to this news?

> ... ***Abraham fell on his face and laughed,*** *and said in his heart, "Shall a child be born to a man who is one hundred years old? And shall Sarah, who is ninety years old, bear a child?"*
> **Genesis 17:17**

He laughed and God went ahead and named the son who was yet to be born; Isaac which means laughter:

> *Then God said: "No, Sarah your wife shall bear you a son, and you shall call his name Isaac; I will establish My covenant with him for an everlasting covenant, and with his descendants after him.*
> **Genesis 17:19**

The news of a hundred-year-old man and his ninety-year-old wife having their first son through normal conception invokes wonder and then laughter. All the stress of the past years diminished into laughter. When Sarah heard the promise for the first time, she also laughed; she wondered whether that was possible!

> And He said, "I will certainly return to you according to the time of life, and behold, Sarah your wife shall have a son."
> (Sarah was listening in the tent door which was behind him.) Now Abraham and Sarah were old, well advanced in age; and Sarah had passed the age of childbearing.
> Therefore, Sarah laughed within herself, saying, "After I have grown old, shall I have pleasure, my lord being old also?"
> And the LORD said to Abraham, "Why did Sarah laugh, saying, 'Shall I surely bear a child, since I am old?'
> Is anything too hard for the LORD? At the appointed time I will return to you, according to the time of life, and Sarah shall have a son."
> But Sarah denied it, saying, "I did not laugh," for she was afraid.
> And He said, "No, but you did laugh!"
> **Genesis 18:10-15**

Sarah might have laughed in doubt because she didn't need a doctor to tell her whether she was fertile or not. Paul described the actual reproductive systems of the couple; Sarah's womb was dead and so was Abraham's body (Romans 4:19). God will revive a naturally impossible condition so you and others can laugh hard but before you get there, be like Abraham. Learn to laugh at yourself and enjoy the wonderful promises God has made. All the tears and sorrows don't demonstrate faith in God; that He can do the naturally impossible.

The real laughter for Sarah came when she cradled her son close to her heart at age 90.

And Sarah said, "God has made me laugh, and all who hear will laugh with me."
She also said, "Who would have said to Abraham that Sarah would nurse children? For I have borne him a son in his old age."
Genesis 21:6-7

Sarah attributed her laughter to God. God wants you to laugh but choose to believe and walk with Him through the trying moments. He says His plans concerning you are good plans; to give you a future and a hope (Jeremiah 29:11). Being hopeful is a life filled with expectation that God who has promised will perfect His will concerning you.

Even though there are many advanced scientific knowhow that aid conception, nothing on earth is guaranteed. Maybe you can afford that but Sarah, Rebecca, Hannah, Manoah's wife and Elizabeth depended solely on the creative power of the word of God. Don't be ashamed of what you can't change about yourself; they can be described differently rather negatively. Like Elizabeth, your joy will be contagious in the end!

Chapter Four

LAUGHTER IS MEDICINAL

A merry heart does good,
like medicine,

Proverbs 17:22a

Laughter Is Healthy

Life experiences can cause you to lose your joy if you don't make time to replenish this joy account. We are sometimes caught up in seasons of disappointment or struggles resulting in loss of joy. Consequently, laughter becomes very rare. But laughter isn't just about jesting or being jovial or joyful, there is more to it. It has curative power according to Proverbs 17:22:

> *A merry heart does good, like medicine,*
> *But a broken spirit dries the bones.*

Whereas a broken spirit affects your body negatively, laughter does you a great deal of good. This well quoted adage; "laughter is the best medicine" certainly has its source from the Bible. A merry heart really does good to one's spirit, soul and body and it's as good as medicine.

In other words, there are spiritual, emotional and physical advantages you can get from being joyful. God didn't overlook anything; even what you don't know that you need have all been supplied in abundance so you can live healthily and happily.

Laughter springs from your emotions but joy from your human spirit. If your source of joy is the Holy Spirit, you can never run out of this scarce commodity. He will replenish it till you have more than you need. Food can excite people yet that is insignificant compared to the joy the Holy Spirit deposits within our hearts:

For the kingdom of God is not eating and drinking,
but righteousness and peace and joy in the Holy Spirit.
Romans 14:17

Joy and laughter come from the Holy Spirit and that affects your whole being; spirit, soul and body.

Laughter Can Boost Your Emotional and Physical Well Being

Are you aware that science has proven why the Bible tells us to laugh because it's good for your health? Laughter is good for your whole being. It reduces stress, fights against depression and unhappiness and helps you develop a positive attitude towards life. Laughter generally puts you in an all-round good mood. This is something people can't pay money to obtain. The opposite of joy is depression and it virtually drains people of the willpower to live but strangely, laughter is priceless. This is true of all the things that are divinely supplied.

When your soul is healthy or hearty, physical health is assured. Stress, depression, sorrow and the like are the sickness of the soul and are expressed through the mind and emotions. Renew your mind constantly by conforming to the word of God. God's word is superior to any counsel man can give you. If forgiving a fellow human being can release you to live fully and stress free, do it. The health of your soul has a direct influence on your physical wellbeing which includes your looks and posture at a glance.

Science has proven that laughter lowers high blood pressure (PB)and positively impacts the cells in your body. Laughter prevents diseases thus, setting you up to live long and healthy. Physical wellbeing is enhanced where one lives a happy life that's full of joy and laughter.

There are people whose lives depend on the prescriptions they have been given by their doctors. They swallow a number of pills of various sizes and colors thrice daily. They believe that they can only survive each day with the help of these medicines and have come this far because of the drugs. Why don't you change your lifestyle by imbibing joy and doses of belly laughs the same way you take your pills? There are stories in this book about individuals with chronic diseases who were made to laugh and got healed totally. You can thrive on the joy of the Lord:

... for this day is holy to our Lord.
Do not sorrow, for the joy of the LORD is your
strength.
Nehemiah 8:10

You can derive strength from the joy you receive from the Lord! This strength is subject to one's needs; emotional or physical. Joy is part of the fruit of the Holy Spirit. Remember that fruits are the make of the mature. Work on yourself to enable you to produce these healthy fruits. Don't let the things of this world have the upper hand when God says you are more than a conqueror. You can overcome when His Spirit actively influences your life.

In fact, medical science tells us that people who laugh boost their immune system because laughter reduces blood pressure. People who laugh regularly are 40% less likely to have a heart attack than people who don't laugh regularly. Laughter triggers the left side of the brain which enables creativity. It helps us to make better decisions. Laughter activates the natural tranquilizers that help us to stay calm and also sleep better. These are certainly some of the priceless benefits of laughter.

Stories about the Healing Effects of Laughter
Many people today suffer from insomnia but you need

to laugh more often. A lady who hadn't slept well in years was constantly taking tranquilizers. She had taken them for so long they hardly worked. She tried everything; dieting, saw different doctors who prescribed different medicines but nothing worked. Finally, one doctor gave her a very unusual prescription. She was told to watch something funny before retiring to bed; a funny movie, a funny video, a funny drama; something that made her laugh. She got better just a month after and she went totally off her medications.

Could it be that you can receive the healing you've been longing for if you just lighten up and learn to laugh more often? The headaches, backaches, migraines, chronic pains and fatigue and even depression would go away if you just take time to laugh and enjoy the life God has given you.

Dodie Osteen was diagnosed with terminal cancer in 1981. This is one of the things she did besides confessing scriptures on healing and medical care; she watched cartoons on television and also had a good laugh. These simple activities released the healing that God had put on the inside and she was healed.

There are too many sicknesses in our world and they are directly related to the fact that we've stopped smiling and laughing. However; there's absolutely free healing power that we can tap. This medicine is available and it's completely free with no side effects; take it as often as you like. Find something funny that makes you laugh out loud. Release that joy out loud.

You activate your natural tranquilizers every time you laugh. It boosts your immune system and reduces your blood pressure. It is tinted with creativity if you stay on this prescription to laugh every day with a happy heart. Having a cheerful mind helps you sleep better. You'll have more energy and make better decisions. Those chronic pain and fatigue will also go away with time.

A lady with a severe case of fibromyalgia went to see a doctor. Her condition was so severe that she spent hours in pain. She had chronic fatigue, no energy; she was in poor health both physically and emotionally. She had gone through tough times and was basically very depressed. When the doctor was about to prescribe the medication, he knew he was only going to deal with the symptoms and not the root cause of the condition.

After he talked with the patient, he realized just how depressed she was hence; the doctor asked her a very interesting question. "How long has it been since you had a good hearty laugh?" The lady thought about it for a moment and she said she hadn't laughed in over 30 years. The doctor then handed over the prescription to the sick woman. She was asked to go and find a very funny movie, funny book and laugh as much as she possibly could. She began to laugh little by little and she got her joy back and so was her energy and health.

The third month, she went back to the doctor for a checkup. The moment she walked in, the doctor could tell that something was different. There was a sparkle in her eyes and a smile on her face. Month after month, she continued to re-learn how to laugh. Eventually, all those diseases left her body.

There's healing power in laughter! When you have a joyful spirit constantly on the inside, health and healing flow constantly. How long has it been since you've had a good hearty laugh? A day, a week, a month, a year, 10 years or more? Make sure you take your laughter medication!

Joel Osteen said whenever his back ached right down the center of his spine, it was an indication of he having had a hard, pressured and tight day. To relieve himself of the pain and tension, he played with his children who made him laugh or watched something funny on television. Invariably, after a few minutes of laughing, that pain totally disappears just like having a massage. However; laughter is much cheaper medicine. Laughter can save you a lot of money. It can save you from buying sleeping pills, tranquilizers and anti-depressing.

Chapter Five

MAINTAIN A JOYOUS MOOD PERSISTENTLY

To everything there is a season,

A time for every purpose under heaven: ...

And a time to laugh; a time to mourn,

Ecclesiastes 3:1, 4

Be Intentional about Laughter

Start making laughter a part of your daily habits and laugh your way to a good and healthy living! To carry out your divine assignment on this earth, you need to stay healthy and this is part of God's plan for your life. People subject the body through needless stress and in the end, they are unable to accomplish anything due to ill-health or premature exit from this earth. God wants you to live long and healthy.

On the average, young children have 300 good belly laughs each day. This gradually decreases as a person grows. A typical adult only experiences 10% good laughs per week! This is because adults have much more responsibilities hence much to think or worry about but the health benefits of laughter are too great to ignore.

Laughter is so important to your health that God factored it into your make-up during creation. There are tremendous benefits if you put on laughter. That's why it's necessary to laugh many times in a day; even if you don't feel like it.

How to Maintain a Joyous Mood

The Bible tells us to *Count it all joy when you fall into various trials,*

James 1:2

Even in circumstances that justify sorrow; even the difficult incidents, we are exhorted to count them all joy. For our own physical, mental and spiritual protection, find joy and something to laugh at even when you are going through the tests of life.

The question is how do you make laughter a regular part of your life, just like physical exercises? In his book, **The God Prescription**, Dr. Avery Jackson prescribes the following:

- Laugh, even when you don't feel like it.
- Watch or listen to comic shows that have no obscenities.
- Read comics in the newspaper.
- Watch funny videos.

Not laughing enough is a choice but that wouldn't be helpful. However, you can also restore your joy by daily reading and meditating on scriptures that talk about joy and laughter. As you follow these exercises, you'll renew your mind hence every shadow of sorrow cast over your soul and body will disappear in Jesus' name. Solomon said:

To everything there is a season,
A time for every purpose under heaven: ...
And a time to laugh; a time to mourn,
Ecclesiastes 3:1, 4

Don't go through life bearing burdens God hasn't placed upon your shoulders. We must discern the times so we can conform to the plans God has for us during the diverse seasons of our lives.

Be intentional about finding some things that will make you laugh. Laugh at yourself; laugh even at the messes you've created. Find something to laugh about while you are out there and by this simple act, you are revitalizing your spirit, soul and body.

Chapter Six

IMBIBE SCRIPTURES ON JOY AND LAUGHTER

Then our mouth was filled with laughter,

And our tongue with singing.

Then they said among the nations,

"The LORD has done great things for them."

Psalm 126:2

Constantly Renew Your Mind

The Bible has a wealth of scriptures on joy and laughter which you must know. They will inform you about God's position on laughter. This has nothing to do with seriousness or the lack of it. Whenever you come under stress, these verses will help you revive yourself. Renewal of mind has to do with conforming negative, fear-infested and doubtful thoughts to God's thoughts and ways.

For I know the plans I have for you," declares the LORD, "plans to prosper you and not to harm you, plans to give you hope and a future.
Jeremiah 29:11-NIV

Joy as well as sadness are choices we make or subject ourselves to daily. There are 30 Bible verses that will easily help you to renew your mind and have the power of laughter restored to you. As you read and meditate, you will begin to see the importance of incorporating laughter into your daily schedules.

Bible Verses that Talk about Joy and Laughter

1. **Genesis 17:17:** *Then Abraham fell on his face and laughed, and said in his heart, "Shall a child be born to a man who is one hundred years old? And shall Sarah, who is*

ninety years old, bear a child?"

2.   **Genesis 21:6** *And Sarah said, "God has made me laugh, and all who hear will laugh with me.*

3.   **Exodus 15:20** *Then Miriam the prophetess, the sister of Aaron, took the timbrel in her hand; and all the women went out after her with timbrels and with dances.*

4.   **2 Samuel 6:14** *Then David danced before the LORD with all his might; and David was wearing a linen ephod.*

5.   **Nehemiah 8:10**   *... for this day is holy to our Lord. Do not sorrow, for the joy of the LORD is your strength.*

6.   **Job 8:21**   *He will yet fill your mouth with laughing, And your lips with rejoicing.*

7.   **Psalm 2:4**   *He who sits in the heavens shall laugh; The LORD shall hold them in derision.*

8.   **Psalm 30:11** *You have turned for me my mourning into dancing;*
You have put off my sackcloth and clothed me with gladness,

9. **Psalm 37:13** *But the Lord just laughs, for he sees their day of judgment coming.*

10. **Psalm 96:12** *Let the fields and their crops burst out with joy! Let the trees of the forest sing for joy.*

11. **Psalm 98:4** *Shout joyfully to the LORD, all the earth; Break forth in song, rejoice, and sing praises.*

12. **Psalm 126:2** *Then our mouth was filled with laughter,*
And our tongue with singing.
Then they said among the nations,
"The LORD has done great things for them."

13. **Proverbs 15:13** *A merry heart makes a cheerful countenance, but by sorrow of the heart the spirit is broken.*

14. **Proverbs 15:15** *All the days of the afflicted are evil, but he who is of a merry heart has a continual feast.*

15. **Proverbs 17:22** *A merry heart does good, like medicine,*

But a broken spirit dries the bones.

16. **Proverbs 31:25** *Strength and honor are her*
    clothing;
    She shall rejoice in time to come.

17. **Ecclesiastes 3:4** *... And a time to laugh;*
    ... And a time to dance;

18. **Ecclesiastes 8:15-NLT** *So I recommend having*
    fun, because there is nothing better for people in
    this world than to eat, drink, and enjoy life. That
    way they will experience some happiness along
    with all the hard work God gives them under the
    sun."

19. **Isaiah 55:12** *The mountains and the hills Shall*
    break forth into singing before you, and all the
    trees of the field shall clap their hands.

20. **Jeremiah 31:13** *"Then shall the virgin rejoice*
    in the dance,
    And the young men and the old, together;
    For I will turn their mourning to joy,
    Will comfort them,
    And make them rejoice rather than sorrow.

21. **Matthew 2:10**
When they saw the star, they rejoiced with exceedingly great joy.

22. **Luke 1:14** *And you will have joy and gladness, and many will rejoice at his birth.*

23. **Luke 2:10** *Then the angel said to them, "Do not be afraid, for behold, I bring you good tidings of great joy which will be to all people.*

24. **Luke 6:21** *Blessed are you who hunger now,*
For you shall be filled.
Blessed are you who weep now,
For you shall laugh.

25. **John 15:11** *These things I have spoken to you, that My joy may remain in you, and that your joy may be full.*

26. **John 16:24** *Until now you have asked nothing in My name. Ask, and you will receive, that your joy may be full.*

27. **John 16:33** *These things I have spoken to you, that in Me you may have peace. In the world you will have tribulation; but be of good cheer, I have overcome the world."*

28. **1 Thessalonians 5:16** *Rejoice always,*

29. **Peter 1:8** *whom having not seen you love. Though now you do not see Him, yet believing, you rejoice with joy inexpressible and full of glory*

30. **1 Peter 4:13** *but rejoice to the extent that you partake of Christ's sufferings, that when His glory is revealed, you may also be glad with exceeding joy.*

Find something funny to laugh about today. Don't wait for it to happen to you accidentally but laugh on purpose and change the course of your life! Laughter is like sunshine; it attracts people towards you. Keep a smiley face even if the going is tough.

Chapter Seven

HEALTH BENEFITS OF LAUGHTER

Rejoice always,

1 Thessalonians 5:16

Laughter Is God's Prescription for Good Health

Dr. Avery Jackson, a neurosurgeon shared some health benefits on the effects of laughter on your spirit, soul and body. He said recent research proves that laughter, in addition to exercises, repairs your body far beyond anything you can do naturally. This can be seen as God's prescription for good health. God built in you some mechanisms to heal your imperfect, earthly body and laughter besides healthy eating habits is one of them. Hence, research only confirms what has been written in Proverbs 22:17:

A merry heart does good, like medicine...

Therefore, there are tremendous health benefits to this simple, priceless and effortless thing as laughter. Any day or time you decide to make laughter a part of your life, you are choosing a healthy and a prolonged life. Some life choices must be intentional because of the stressful things that we face each day which deprive us of laughter. Whenever you choose to laugh there are health benefits money can't pay for.

The good news is that you can make a decision to laugh every day and as you do, you will rake in these five awesome health benefits for your spirit, soul and body. What are these health benefits of laughter?

1. Laughter Increases Your Blood Flow

Whenever you really have a good laugh, you are getting healthier! Science reveals that laughter actually improves your blood flow. When your blood flow improves, it triggers some positives effects in your body:

- It reduces your stress hormones,
- It lowers your blood pressure and
- It activates your immune system.

That is the reason why Proverbs 17:22 says, *"A merry heart does good, like medicine"* and this is more or less preventive in that it boosts your immune system. Poor blood flow is the root cause of many diseases. Poor blood flow increases inflammation which is the root cause of other major diseases.

Exercise is also a key element in ensuring healthy blood flow especially for people with sedentary lifestyles. Exercises and laughter will enable you to increase blood flow to the brain. They enable God's healing mechanism to be effected to prevent diseases. They also repair or prevent neurodegenerative disorders like Parkinson's disease and Alzheimer's.

There are amazing health benefits for people who make laughter a habit. Remarkably your body benefits just from laughter. Studies have shown that stress hormones like adrenaline and epinephrine drop 70% just from anticipating a good laugh and mood-elevating hormones called endorphins get a boost whenever you laugh. So if you want to experience divine health in your spirit, soul and body, get your body moving and get your daily belly laughs!

2. Laughter Reduces Pain

The second benefit is laughter reduces pain. If you have really experienced serious pain, all you desire is how you can make it go away. The doctors certainly will prescribe varieties of toxic painkillers that may end up destroying other body organs especially, your kidneys. Because people are seeking quick relief from pain, they are put on highly addictive prescription painkillers. Some people end up addicted to these destructive painkillers.

Ironically, the last thing you will ever think while in pain is laughter which is God's best option for you.

Though pain relief is often necessary, God has His own prescription for pain. Laughter acts as a natural painkiller just as exercises. Both work in the same way as a prescription or painkiller in the way they chemically affect the cell receptors in your brain and body. That's God's awesome way!

According to Dr. Jackson, God made the naturally occurring hormone dopamine to relieve pain and we can boost our dopamine levels through exercise and laughter which reduce pain naturally. An article in the *New England Medical Journal* stated that 10 minutes of belly laughter can relieve pain for up to two hours!

These two exercises can be combined with faith declarations (speaking and standing on God's Word or promises) for healing. By these, you can take control of what may seem like an out-of-control situation. Whatever the health condition is or the diagnosis, the Bible says a merry heart does good, like medicine .   Spend some hours every day watching and listening to episodes that will excite good laughter. There are many Bible verses that assure us that healing is divine and adding laughter and exercise to your routine is clearly beneficial.

3. Laughter Prevents Diseases

It has already been stated that laughter increases blood flow. From this comes immune boosters, etc. Hence; the benefits of laughter don't stop at simply reducing pain but it can prevent diseases as well. Research has revealed that laughter can improve your health and prevent diseases by:

- Lowering blood pressure,
- Releasing muscle tension,
- Increasing feel-good hormones (dopamine, endorphins),
- Decreasing stress hormones,
- Boosting your immune system,
- Burning calories and
- Giving you an overall sense of well-being.

It may interest you to know that laughter has been found to:

- Reduce tumors,
- Increase the effectiveness of cancer treatments, and
- Lengthen the lives of cancer patients.

4. Laughter Improves Emotional Health

In addition research has found that emotional health is strongly connected to physical health because, as Dr. Jackson explains, Emotional issues affect how you see the world, which will, in turn, impact your body and emotions. Part of your emotional health comes from how you process past situations. When you experience emotional trauma as a child, it often leads to lingering pain and unhappiness in adult life. The reason is there is a direct link between what you've been through and your perception of things as an adult.

Without the help of the Lord or not walking in the light of the truth of God's Word, those traumas can cause you much. The way to emotional health is through the Lord Jesus Christ being your Savior and Lord. Jesus becomes your source of strength and joy in addition to bearing the fruit of the Spirit which was released to you when you got born again. Joy is a big part of pushing the reset button on emotional trauma which must be operated by faith and the way to do so is laughter. When you choose to laugh, you choose the joy of the Lord which also positively affects your spirit, soul and body. That's who you are really meant to be in Christ Jesus.

Laughter is a factor of emotional healing. Whenever you feel gloomy, dejected or miserable, make yourself laugh. Always try to combine laughter with physical and spiritual exercises. Sing and dance or pray in the spirit while doing other physical exercises. Try also to get as many belly laughs each day as possible. By this, you obey God by making Him your joy and invariably your strength.

5. Laughter Strengthens Your Spirit

God is spirit and He relates with our human spirits. The Lord ministers strength to your spirit, soul and body. Dr. Jackson said that, "There is an anointing that comes from joy that strengthens you when there is no strength." The ability to laugh from an overflow of joy in the Spirit has incredible spiritual benefit. When you laugh, you defy the devil's ability to bring sadness, anxiety or hopelessness and the like into your life. You laugh at his lack of authority.

Instead of dreading the future due to uncertainties, with laughter which is an expression of faith, you *"shall rejoice in time to come"* (Proverbs 31:25). It is an error to be in Christ and allow the pressures and stress of this life to get you down.

Chapter Eight

QUOTES ON LAUGHTER

This chapter gives you some people's opinions on laughter. These quotes only buttress the points already stated in this book and which have been confirmed by research that laughter is God's medium to keep you sound and healthy. Slowly read, enjoy and digest the quotes:

1.   I love people who make me laugh. I honestly think it's the thing I like most, to laugh. It cures a multitude of ills. It's probably the most important thing for a person. **- Audrey Hepburn**

2.   Always laugh when you can, it is cheap medicine. **- Lord Byron**

3.   There is nothing in the world so irresistibly contagious as laughter and good humor. **- Charles Dickens, A Christmas Carol**

4.   "If you wish to glimpse inside a human soul and get to know a man, don't bother analyzing his ways of being silent, of talking, of weeping, of seeing how much he is moved by noble ideas; you will get better

results if you just watch him laugh. If he laughs well, he's a good man."
— **Fyodor Dostoevsky**

5. "The human race has only one really effective weapon and that is laughter." — **Mark Twai**

6. Among those whom I like or admire, I can find no common denominator, but among those whom I love, I can; all of them make me laugh. — **W.H. Auden**

7. Laughter and tears are both responses to frustration and exhaustion. I myself prefer to laugh, since there is less cleaning to do afterward. — **Kurt Vonne**

8. The ability to laugh at myself takes me from being a victim to being a victor - **Annie Keys**

9. The most wasted of all days is one without laughter
-CC Cummings

10. I am especially glad of the divine gift of laughter: It has made the world human and lovable, despite all its pain and wrong. - **W.E.B. Du Bois**

11. A good laugh is a mighty good thing, a rather too scarce a good thing. - **Herman Melville**

12. A good laugh recharges your battery.

13. A good laugh heals a lot of hurts.

14. Laugh as much as you breathe and love as much as you live -**Johnny Depp**

15. Laugh and be happy and the world will smile with you.

16. Always find a reason to laugh. It may not add years to your life but it will surely add life to your years.

17. Life is better when you are laughing.

18. Laughing is a weapon of mass construction.

19. Laughing is the best exercise.

20. Laughter is the best medicine.

21. Laughter is the language of the soul.

22. Laughter is a good exercise. It is jogging on the inside.

-Pablo Neroda
23. To laugh at yourself is to love yourself.

24. The secret of long life is laughter. The secret of a long-lasting relationship is laughing together.

25. The earth laughs in flowers.
     - Ralph Waldo Emerson

Chapter Nine

TESTIMONIES ON THE POSITIVE EFFECTS OF LAUGHTER

Laughter, the Secret to Long Life

Joel Osteen shared an experience. He met a lady in the visitor's lounge years ago after service. She was 96 and was as healthy as can be. Her mind was sharp, her skin was beautiful and her eyes were bright. What stuck out was how happy she was. She knew no stranger, everybody was her best friend and she was hugging all the people in the line. I mean she was a breath of fresh air and she was wearing a really bright colorful fancy dress. After talking and hugging, Joel said in passing that: "I believe when I'm 96, I will be just like". She leaned over and whispered into his ears that: "just don't wear the dress". I thought no wonder she was so healthy: she still had a sense of humor and still knew how to laugh.

Think about all those years of healing flowing through her body whenever she laughed. Realize you will get older and eventually die. Make up your mind to enjoy the number of years God is giving you by staying joyous; have a smile on your face and laugh heartily often.

Laughter, the Remedy for Depression

Dr. Stewart Brown, the founder of the National Institute of Play in America became interested in the effects of laughter in our lives when he was to investigate the tower shootings on the University of Texas campus in 1966. After talking with the young man who shot and killed all those people, one thing that stuck out was that the young man never played as a child. He grew up in a dysfunctional home where laughter or even playing was nonexistent.

Dr. Brown then proceeded to investigate the other inmates on death row in Texas that year. He discovered that not one of them had a normal childhood. None of them could remember ever laughing, playing or having a good time. Dr. Brown deduced that the opposite of play is not work but depression. He said that it is healthy to laugh and have fun. Proverbs 17:22 says: *'a happy heart is like good medicine and a cheerful mind works healing'*. Form a good nature that's full of joy; take time to laugh and play. This is like taking good medicine and it will help you to stay healthy.

Laughter Restores and Strengthens Relationships

Laughter releases the body's natural medicine. It brings physical healing as well as strengthens your relationships. Friends, it is great to have laughter in your home. One thing the enemy can't stand is the sound of laughter. He can't stand the sounds of husbands, wives and family members having fun together. He's there to cause much strife, tension and pressure such that we never have any joy in our homes.

Many people fall into this trap. Fill your whole house with joy since laughter is contagious. The secret of a healthy marriage are two things; respect and laughter. Don't ever stop laughing together! Keep your home filled with fun. Take your relationship to a new level by getting some joy back in the home. Remember the things you used to do together you were courting and how you used to have fun and laugh together

A couple were struggling in their marriage. These were good people who loved each other but a lot of pressure coming from a lot of issues started pulling them apart. They decided to take one night a week to watch a funny movie together and laughed together. Something so simple had a major impact and changed the atmosphere of their home. Laughter brought newness into their relationship. If you can laugh together, it will help you to stay together.

Laughter as a Magnet Pulls Others towards You

Laughter doesn't only reduce tension but it draws people towards you. It helps bring down the walls that so often separates. You can be the total stranger but if you ever laugh together, the defenses come down.

I found that when you are good natured, you know how to laugh. You are friendly and smile, you will see more of God's favor. Someone shared a story where something he should have paid for was offered for free because he was full of smiles. The person was told: "we need more happy people around here!" Spend your day smiling and laughing with everybody you see. Choose to be joyful because it draws people towards you but when you are all serious, all work and no play, it pushes people away.

Be willing to laugh at yourself. Don't be so uptight, stiff, defensive and insecure. If you do something that's dumb or you make a mistake, laugh about it. Do you know that every time you laughed, you got healthier and stronger? However; these days people hardly laugh even with their children. They are too stressed up. The news shows that these are troubling times but you can believe the opposite. The more difficult it is, the more you need to activate your joy. The more pressure you feel, the more you need to look for opportunities to laugh.

Laugh Your Way to Victory

Every other minute you hear doom and gloom; that it's going to be so bad or going to get much worse, if you are not careful, you will fall into that trap of thinking this isn't the time to enjoy your life. However, you need to activate your joy. Job 5: 22 says:
> *'at destruction and famine we should laugh'*

How can you laugh at famine or difficulties? It is easier to lose your joy during tough times and when you lose your joy, you lose your strength. When you don't have strength you will be defeated and you will catch diseases when you are not strong. You shouldn't have your immune system down. When you are tired, worried or stressed out, God has a solution; He says in difficulties cheer up. Choose to laugh your way to victory; to better health and more energy.

In Psalms 2:4 God sits in the heavens laughing! He is not worried about the economy or upset about His enemies. God's throne is full of joy. God is laughing because He can see the destruction of the enemy coming. In other words, the reason why God laughs is because He knows the end of the story. God knows the final outcome and the good news is, God always causes us to triumph.

- By faith, God has destined you to win. (Romans 8:37),
- God is supplying all your needs (Philippians 4:19),
- God is healing of your diseases (Isaiah 53:5),
- God is fighting your battles for you (Exodus 14:13),
- He is your vindicator, your way maker and deliverer (Romans 11:26),
- He has given you the desires of your heart (Psalm 37:4).

When God gave Abraham a promise that he was going to have a child, naturally it was impossible but what Abraham did first was to laugh. It was a laughter of faith. Abraham knew that the supernatural God could do it.

Oftentimes, when God puts a promise in your heart, it looks impossible. Maybe you are sick and God says, you are going to be well. You are struggling financially but God says, He will give you overflow and prosper you. Your family is falling apart but God says, He is going to bring them back together.

Your mind sometimes says; it's never going to happen or you'll never see your dreams come to fulfillment but just remember to do like Abraham did. No matter how you feel, you need to let out the laughter of faith. God has already worked it out; He's already arranged things in your favor and it's just a matter of time before these promises come to pass. You can laugh by faith knowing you are in a fixed fight.

Get into the habit of taking your laughter medicines on a regular basis. Find some reasons to laugh; look for opportunities. Just know that you can laugh by faith. Remember to stir up the joy; stir up the healing that's within you. When you keep a happy heart and a cheerful mind, you are not only going to enjoy your life more but you are going to see healing flow through you in a new way. You shall be free from chronic illnesses, chronic fatigue and things that have been holding you back.

You'll see your relationships go to a new level because God will pour His favor upon you in a greater measure just like Abraham. Note that every promise, dream, desire God has put in your heart; no matter how impossible it looks, God will bring it to pass. Just maintain a cheerful heart and keep on laughing heartily. Amen

REFERENCES

1. Dr. Avery M. Jackson *The God Prescription*; Our Heavenly Father's Plan for Spiritual, Mental, and Physical Health

2. Kenneth Copeland Ministries 25 Scriptures about Laughter and Joy

3. Joel Osteen The Healing Power of Laughter -Youtube

Printed in Great Britain
by Amazon

19465180R00045